Behind Media

Internet

Sally Morgan

www.heinemann.co.uk/library

Visit our website to find out more information about **Heinemann Library** books.

To order:

☎ Phone 44 (0) 1865 888066

📄 Send a fax to 44 (0) 1865 314091

💻 Visit the Heinemann Bookshop at www.heinemann.co.uk/library to browse our catalogue and order online.

First published in Great Britain by Heinemann Library, Halley Court, Jordan Hill, Oxford, OX2 8EJ,
a division of Reed Educational and Professional Publishing Ltd.
Heinemann is a registered trademark of Reed Educational and Professional Publishing Ltd.

OXFORD MELBOURNE AUCKLAND
JOHANNESBURG BLANTYRE GABORONE
IBADAN PORTSMOUTH NH (USA) CHICAGO

Designed by Paul Davies and Associates
Originated by Ambassador Litho Ltd.
Printed in Hong Kong/China

ISBN 0 431 11463 3
05 04 03 02 01
10 9 8 7 6 5 4 3 2 1

British Library Cataloguing in Publication Data

Morgan, Sally
  Internet. - (Behind Media)
  1.Internet - (Computer network) - Juvenile literature
  I.Title
  004.6'78

Acknowledgements
The Publishers would like to thank the following for permission to reproduce photographs: 2000
Dreamworks, Pathe and Aardman: p11; BBC: p21; Niall Benvie/Calumet: p24; Borders: p30; Bridgeman:
p40; Trevor Clifford: pp26, 32; Ecoscene: p25; Google: p36; Hollywood.com: p8; Image Bank: p4; Intuition
design; pp15, 16, 29; R.W. Jones/Corbis: pp13, 23; NASA: p45; Oxfam International: p6; Panos: p44;
Photomosaic TM © 2000 by Robert Silvers: p5; Shoot Photographic: p20; Stone: p41, Daniel Bosler p27, P
Crowther/S Carter p31, Peter Poulides p42; TEK Image/Science Photo Library: p43; United Nations: p8;
WWF: p18.

Cover photograph reproduced with permission of The Stock Market.

Our thanks to Chris Jennings for his comments in the preparation of this book.

Every effort has been made to contact copyright holders of any material reproduced in this book.
Any omissions will be rectified in subsequent printings if notice is given to the Publisher.

Trademarks/Registered Trademarks
Computer hardware and software brand names mentioned in this book are protected by their respective
trademarks and are acknowledged.

Contents

Any words appearing in the text in bold, **like this**, are explained in the Glossary.

What is the Internet?

The Internet is a word that is on everyone's lips. So what is the Internet? It is a huge global network of computers, with millions of machines connected together along cables, via radio waves or even by satellite links. The Internet is used to send packets of information from one computer to another, anywhere in the world, usually in less than a second. These packets of information can be likened to electronic postcards that bear a delivery address. If you put the right address on a packet, and give it to any computer that is connected to part of the Internet, each computer works out which cable to send it down next, so that the packet reaches the correct destination.

The Internet gives the family access to all sorts of information, from train timetables to government legislation, and to leisure activities such as on-line shopping and chatting.

What is the difference between the Net and the Web?

If the Internet or 'Net' is made up of computers connected together, the **World Wide Web** or 'Web' is a collection of documents, sounds, videos, **digital** photographs and information of all sorts, all connected by **HTML** links (see page 5). The Web exists because of programs that communicate between computers on the Net. The Web could not exist without the Net. The Web makes the Internet useful because people are interested in information and don't really want or need to know how the computers communicate.

This book looks at just one aspect of the Internet in detail – **websites**. It will examine how an organization, such as a wildlife charity, might go about setting up a new website, the types of features that it could include on the pages and the people and skills needed to carry out the project.

In the beginning

The origins of the Internet date back to the early 1960s. The US Department of Defense's Advanced Research Projects Agency (ARPA) developed a small network of computers, called ARPANET, which was like a high-speed digital post office, passing small packets of information from one computer to another. It allowed scientists to share **data** and access remote computers. In 1973, ARPA started research on a project called Internetting, which developed technologies to allow different networks to communicate with each other. But it took around ten years for scientists to develop TCP/IP – a common technology to be used on all computers on the network. It was the work of an Englishman, Tim Berners-Lee, that turned the Internet into the World Wide Web, which is the heart of the Internet as we know it today. He developed the concept of **Uniform Resource Locators (URLs)**. These can be thought of as Internet addresses that allow any document on the Web to be easily indicated and retrieved. Since these early beginnings, the Internet has changed out of all recognition.

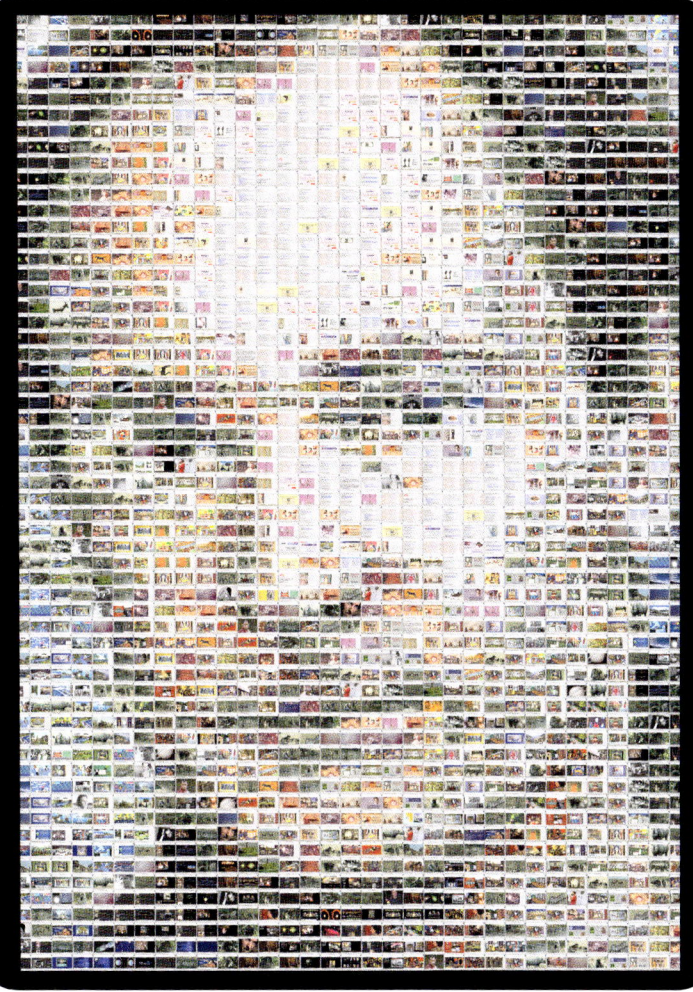

This picture of Tim Berners-Lee is made from hundreds of computer screens. Tim Berners-Lee is probably the most important figure in the history of the World Wide Web. He was the first to work on the concept of web pages and addresses as a way of locating information.

Key words

Here are a few definitions of some of the key words associated with the Internet. The Internet is always spelt with a capital I and it refers to the global network of computers that are all connected together using the TCP/IP **protocol**. A protocol is a standard that specifies how the computers on the network interact with each other. The World Wide Web or Web is the collection of interconnecting web pages that form a global source of information.

Web pages are written using HyperText Markup Language (HTML), a language that uses text and a defined set of commands (known as **tags**) to create most of what you see on a web page. The tags have two distinct functions. They either define the text display style (whether it is in bold or italic, and so on), or make the text act as a link to another page, a picture, or an **animation** or even play a sound or run a complete program. A web page is an Internet 'document' that can be accessed by Internet users with an HTML **browser** such as Microsoft ® Internet Explorer ® or Netscape ® Navigator. By providing the browser with a unique address, or Uniform Resource Locator (URL), you open the page pointed to by that address.

Going on-line

Every year, the number of people accessing the Internet increases. It is changing our way of life by making communication so much easier. Sending an **e-mail** to somebody on the other side of the world is quicker, cheaper and more reliable than sending a letter. There are **on-line** newspapers and news services that bring you up-to-the minute news 24 hours a day. It takes seconds to find the times of trains, buses and flights, eliminating the need to spend time queuing on telephone help-lines. You can even buy the travel tickets on-line. The Web is also changing our shopping habits. Now, at the click of a button, you can order goods to be delivered directly to your home, sometimes within hours.

Just a few years ago, many companies could only market their services in their local area, or possibly nation-wide. Nowadays, the Internet makes it simple for companies, whether large or small, to market their services world-wide. It is truly a global marketplace.

Why is a website important?

The Internet is all about communication and information. It allows people, companies, governments and charities to communicate with the public. For a company, a **website** is like a shop window, and can be a powerful means of communicating with clients. A simple site can provide information about the company's services and background, as well as give profiles on key members of staff.

Many companies have **e-commerce** sites which advertise the goods that they sell and offer facilities to buy these goods on-line. Governments set up websites to communicate with their citizens and tell them about their policies, new laws, the work of the different governmental departments and their plans.

So why do charities want a website? Charities need to communicate with the public in the same way as a government or commercial company. Charities use their websites to inform the public about their work. The site may attract visitors who decide to become members and it may help the charity raise money by selling goods. Charities often rely on public donations as a means of raising the money they need to carry out their work. They can raise money by organizing activities such as sponsored walks, sales and direct mail. Fund-raising ability is limited by the level of public awareness. Larger charities, such as the Save the Children Fund and the RSPCA, are well known and have a much easier job of persuading people to donate money. But smaller charities, especially those that work in just one part of the country or have a limited function, for example a small animal sanctuary or a charity raising money for research into a rare disease, find fund-raising more difficult. People are often not even aware of their existence. Raising awareness may involve sending letters to local people or doing publicity stunts that are reported in the local papers. By setting up a website they can not only make themselves accessible to many more people at a much lower cost, but can also make it easy for people who are interested to get in contact.

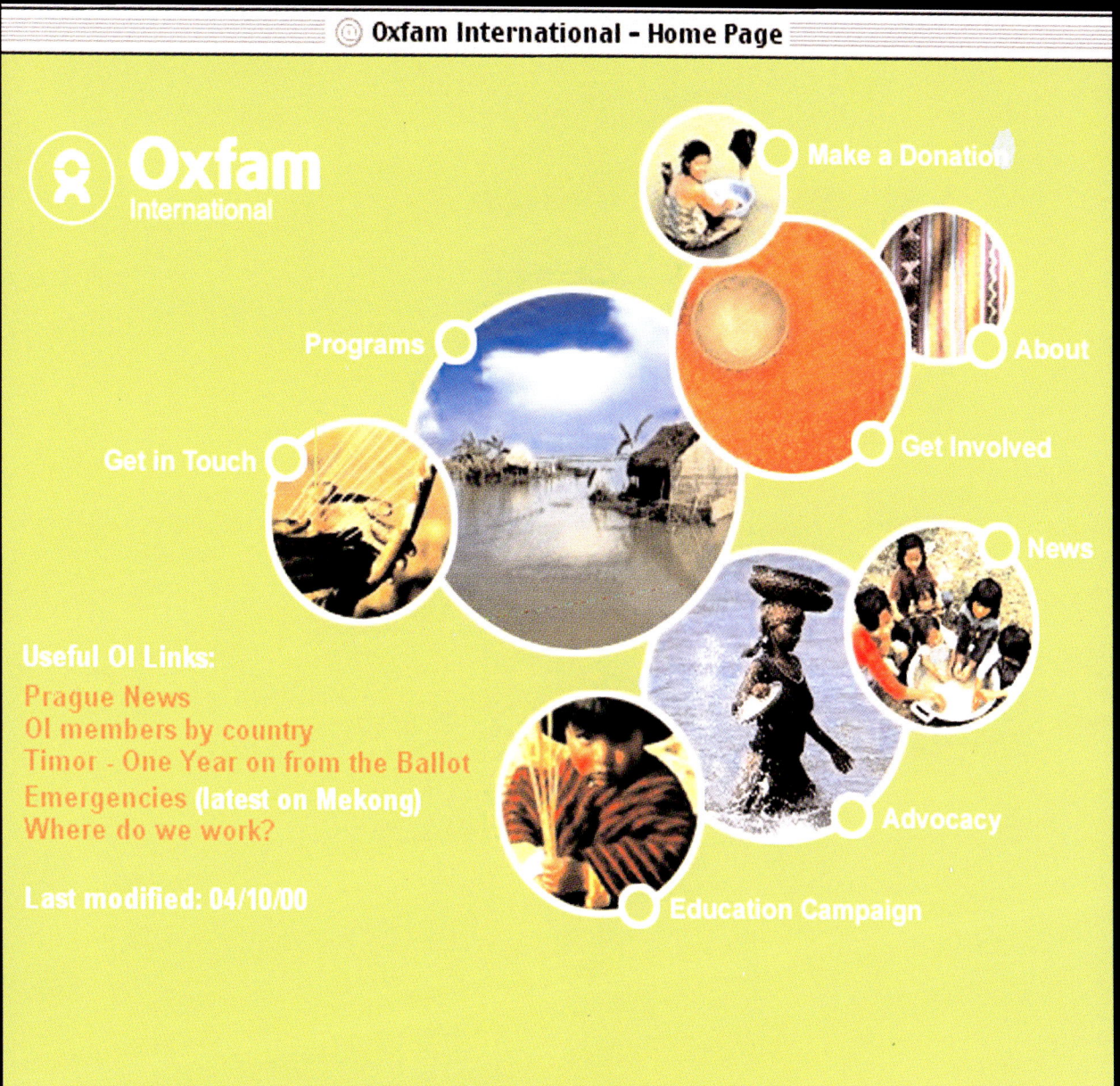

Oxfam
International

Make a Donation

About

Get Involved

News

Programs

Get in Touch

Advocacy

Education Campaign

Useful OI Links:

Prague News
OI members by country
Timor - One Year on from the Ballot
Emergencies (latest on Mekong)
Where do we work?

Last modified: 04/10/00

The Internet allows charities, such as Oxfam, to be accessible to a much greater audience. The costs of setting up a website are often considerably less than the costs of advertising campaigns and mail shots.

Technical tips

To access the Internet, a user needs a computer with a **modem**, a telephone line and an **Internet Service Provider (ISP)**. An ISP is a company that provides you with a gateway to the Internet. Once you are on-line, you can send people e-mail, take part in a discussion group, chat with people all over the world, buy goods and find out all sorts of information.

Building the Foundations

Good design

When building a **website** from scratch, it is important to remember what makes a good design. A well-designed website creates a good impression with visitors, who may make repeat visits.

Easy navigation

Visitors must be able to move around the site with ease, so the **navigation** has to be simple and easy to follow. The information should be interesting and appear quickly. Research shows that if the time taken to start to display **downloaded** information is longer than just a few seconds, visitors leave the site after viewing only a page or two. The content should be up-to-date and changed regularly, so that people are encouraged to make repeat visits.

These two screens show the difference in approach taken by web designers. The screen on the left shows a website about celebrities and is aimed at a young audience. The United Nations page on the right is text only. Fancy graphics and animations would slow down the access time, so these elements of web design are avoided.

HOLLYWOOD.COM
Isn't it time you went Hollywood!

Click Here for the best in UnderGround entertainment.

HOLLYWOOD.COM NETWORK: Broadway.com | Movietickets.com | Musicsite.com | About Us

HOME | NEWS | MOVIES | CELEBS | TV | SHOWTIMES | SHOPPING | MUSIC | MULTIMEDIA | INTERNATIONAL

news
- Dixie Chicks Clean House
- Which Winger Got Clipped?
- Russell Crowe: $20 Mil Man?
- Japan's Favorite Son: Lennon
- Lew Irwin Studio Briefings
- Liz Smith Gossip
- Sandy Kenyon's Hollywood Update
- Broadway.com Buzz

ARE WOMEN ON TOP?

Some of Hollywood's biggest actresses --

movie *showtimes* & tickets
enter your zip code:
Find

multimedia

video exclusives
Bruce Willis
Dark Angel
Remember the Titan
The Exorcist
More...

box office

new this week
Digimon: The Movie
Get Carter
Bamboozled
Meet The Parents
More...

now showing
Girlfight
Remember The Titans
Beautiful
Best In Show
More...

coming soon
Dr. T and the Women
The Contender
Ladies Man

About the United Nations / History

History of the UN | Milestones | Major Achievements | 50th Anniversary

The name "United Nations" was devised by United States President Franklin D. Roosevelt and was first used in the "Declaration by United Nations" of 1 January 1942, during the Second World War, when representatives of 26 nations pledged their Governments to continue fighting together against the Axis Powers.

The United Nations Charter was drawn up by the representatives of 50 countries at the United Nations Conference on International Organization, which met at San Francisco from 25 April to 26 June 1945. Those delegates deliberated on the basis of proposals worked out by the representatives of China, the Soviet Union, the United Kingdom and the United States at Dumbarton Oaks in August-October 1944. The Charter was signed on 26 June 1945 by the representatives of the 50 countries. Poland, which was not represented at the Conference, signed it later and became one of the original 51 Member States.

The United Nations officially came into existence on 24 October 1945, when the Charter had been ratified by China, France, the Soviet Union, the United Kingdom, the United States and by a majority of other signatories. United Nations Day is celebrated on 24 October each year.

Nations, Sales No. E.95.I.31.

Who will visit the site?

The charity has to identify its target audience, as this will be one of the most important factors when deciding on the look and feel of the site. The following questions need to be answered:

- ✡ Who will visit the site?
- ✡ What age group does the website want to attract?
- ✡ What will the visitor want from the site?

Obviously, a website aimed at a young audience needs a lively design with exciting **graphics**, **animations** and other **interactive** features. In contrast, a website designed to provide important information, such as government policy, will need a more serious appearance with fewer graphics, as most visitors will visit with the sole purpose of accessing information. Fancy graphics would only irritate the user by making the pages slower to load.

This charity website will need to appeal to a wide range of age groups and people from different backgrounds, so it will have to balance the needs of the young with those of older visitors. This could be achieved by having different areas on the website, with one especially for the younger visitor.

Nowadays, people can buy software packages to design their web pages, so it is relatively easy for an individual to put together a website and publish it from home. However, large companies and organizations such as charities need to put together a professional site that can cope with thousands of visitors each day. This means that they usually have to employ a team of people to build and manage their websites.

Designing for the visually impaired

Millions of visually impaired people access the Internet. A computer is a superb tool for a visually impaired person. **On-line** information provides many benefits compared with printed information. It is easy for people with poor eyesight to increase the font to a size that suits them. The Internet also allows them to work from home and still be in contact with the office. However, modern web design, with its emphasis on visual content, is making it increasingly difficult for the visually impaired to read the screen. The use of **encoded HTML** prevents the user from making changes, such as increasing the size of the text. A text-based screen is easy to access, as the text is fed straight to a screen reader, but text arranged in columns causes problems for text converters. Also, many websites do not have alternative text for images, that is a brief line of text describing the image or the function of the image. Train timetables, for example, are sometimes displayed as graphics that cannot be converted to text.

On the job

A web marketing manager is responsible for getting as many visitors to a website as possible. First they have to identify their target market – the type of users who will visit the site – and then set up a marketing strategy to attract these users. They may check out the websites owned by the competition and carry out market research. Armed with this information, they choose the most appropriate places to advertise the website. Once the marketing campaign is under way, they will evaluate its success and compare their performance to that of competitors.

The importance of a domain name

All computers on the Internet that contain information for **downloading** are identified by a unique number, called an Internet Protocol (IP) address. These addresses are used to route information around the Internet, but, while they are perfect for computers, they are not exactly easy for people to remember. This is where **domain names** come in. A domain name is a familiar, easy to remember name, that corresponds to the location of information on the Internet. The Domain Name Service (DNS) on the Internet 'translates' the domain name into an IP address, and so sends information to the correct place.

The structure of a domain name

A domain name is usually divided into two or three parts. Let us assume someone wants to set up a charity called 'Elephant Aid'. They would like to use the name *www.elephantaid.org*. The *www* part simply refers to the **World Wide Web**. The *org* bit indicates the top-level domain, to which the domain name belongs. The word *elephantaid* makes the domain name unique. The top-level domains are fixed and there are several alternatives:

Advertisers frequently insert a website address on advertisements in magazines and on billboards. A short web address is much easier to remember than a telephone number or mailing address.

- ✡ *.org* is used by non-profit-making organizations such as charities
- ✡ *.com* or *.co* is used for commercial sites
- ✡ *.edu* is for educational sites
- ✡ *.ac* is for academic sites, such as universities
- ✡ *.net* represents a network, and is often used by **ISPs**
- ✡ *.gov* is used for government organizations
- ✡ *.mil* is for military sites.

Due to the shortage of domain names at the top level, some new top-level domains, such as .shop, .web and .info are awaiting approval.

FROM THE CREATORS OF WALLACE AND GROMIT

CHICKEN RUN

www.chickenrun.co.uk

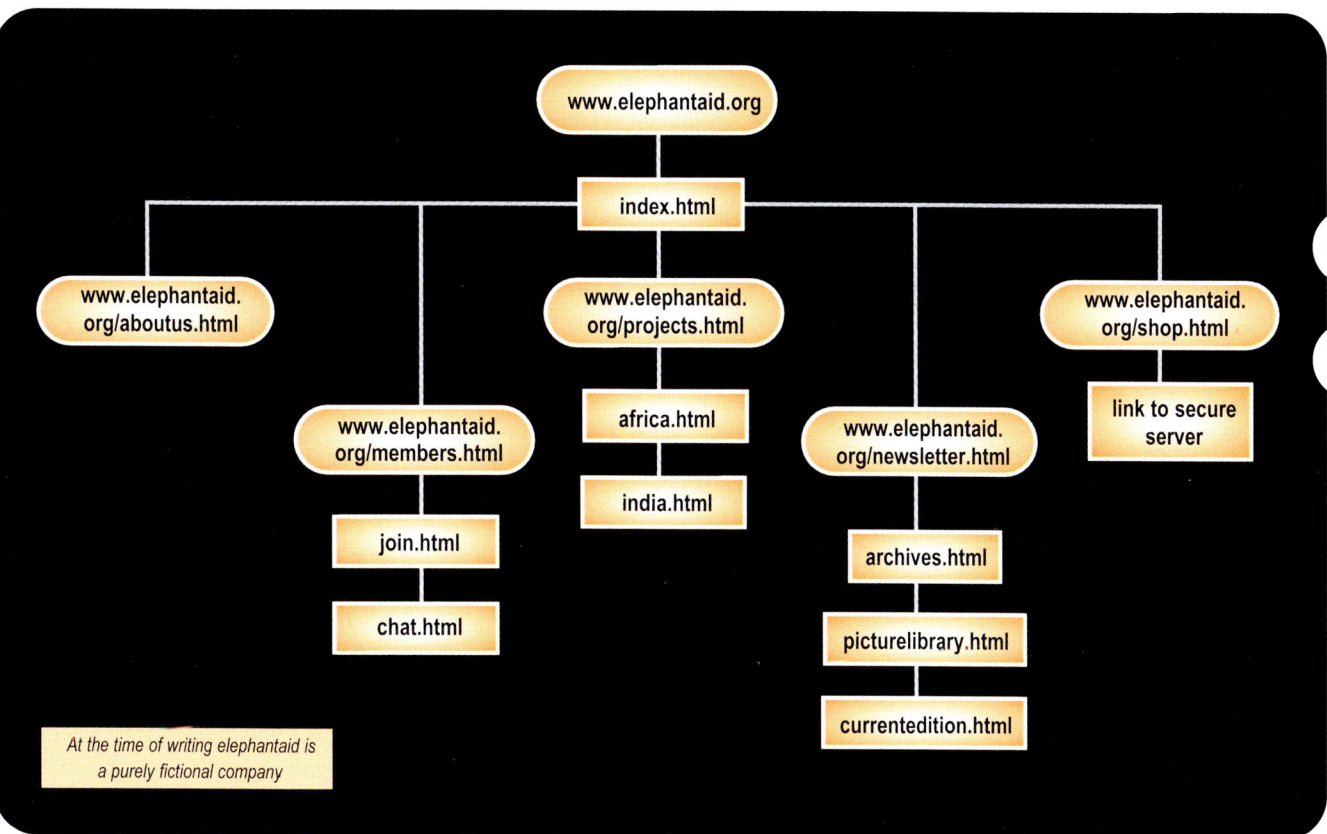

At the time of writing elephantaid is a purely fictional company

If an organization is based solely in one country, it may choose a domain name that indicates the country of origin. For example, *www.elephantaid.org.uk* would indicate an organization based in the United Kingdom. Each country has its own suffix of two letters, such as *au* for Australia and *fr* for France. The country of origin always goes at the end of the domain name, after the top-level domain.

Domain names must be unique, so only one person or organization can have a particular domain name. The first person to register a name gets the right to use that name. If the chosen domain name has already been taken, another has to be selected. A similar one can be achieved by, for example, adding a hyphen between two words or adding another word. For example, *www.elephantaid.org* could be changed to *www.elephant-aid.org*.

Registering the domain name

In order to get a domain name, the charity will use the services of any one of the many registrars who offer domain name services. To register a domain name, they will be asked to provide the registrar with the various contact and technical information that makes up the registration. The registrar will then keep records of the contact information and submit the technical information to a central directory known as the 'registry'. This registry provides other computers on the Internet with the address translation necessary to send them **e-mail** or to find their **website**.

Once a domain name is registered, Internet users only need to type the domain name in order to be taken to the web page. On many web **browsers**, you can see that an address translation has occurred because an IP address is shown at the bottom of the screen. Go to a different domain, and the IP address will change.

This simple diagram shows how the different pages in a website could be named and linked. By typing the address www.elephantaid.org, a visitor is taken straight to the **home page***. Visitors can go directly to a particular page on a website if they know the page address.*

Preparing web space

*Most people gain access to the Internet through their ISP, using **modems** on computers, mobile phones or TVs. They are then routed via many other computers to the computer that stores the information that they require. Most servers are protected by **firewalls** so that people cannot gain unauthorized access to the information.*

Now that the charity has a **domain name**, it needs to set up its **website**. To do this, it needs web space on a computer that is connected to the Internet. Large organizations and some charities have their own computer, known as a **server**, which is linked to the Internet. But this is an expensive business as the server, and often a second, back-up computer, have to be kept running 24 hours a day. The organizations also have to pay for the rental or purchase of the **data** communication lines, called 'pipes', to the Internet. Smaller organizations, and most charities, rent web space from an **ISP** or other computer company and share links into the Internet. ISPs include **on-line** service companies such as AOL, Compuserve and Freeserve as well as many smaller independent companies whose servers are directly connected to the Internet. The chosen ISP will be responsible for managing the computers and communications links and keeping the website on-line. Most provide web space as part of their service.

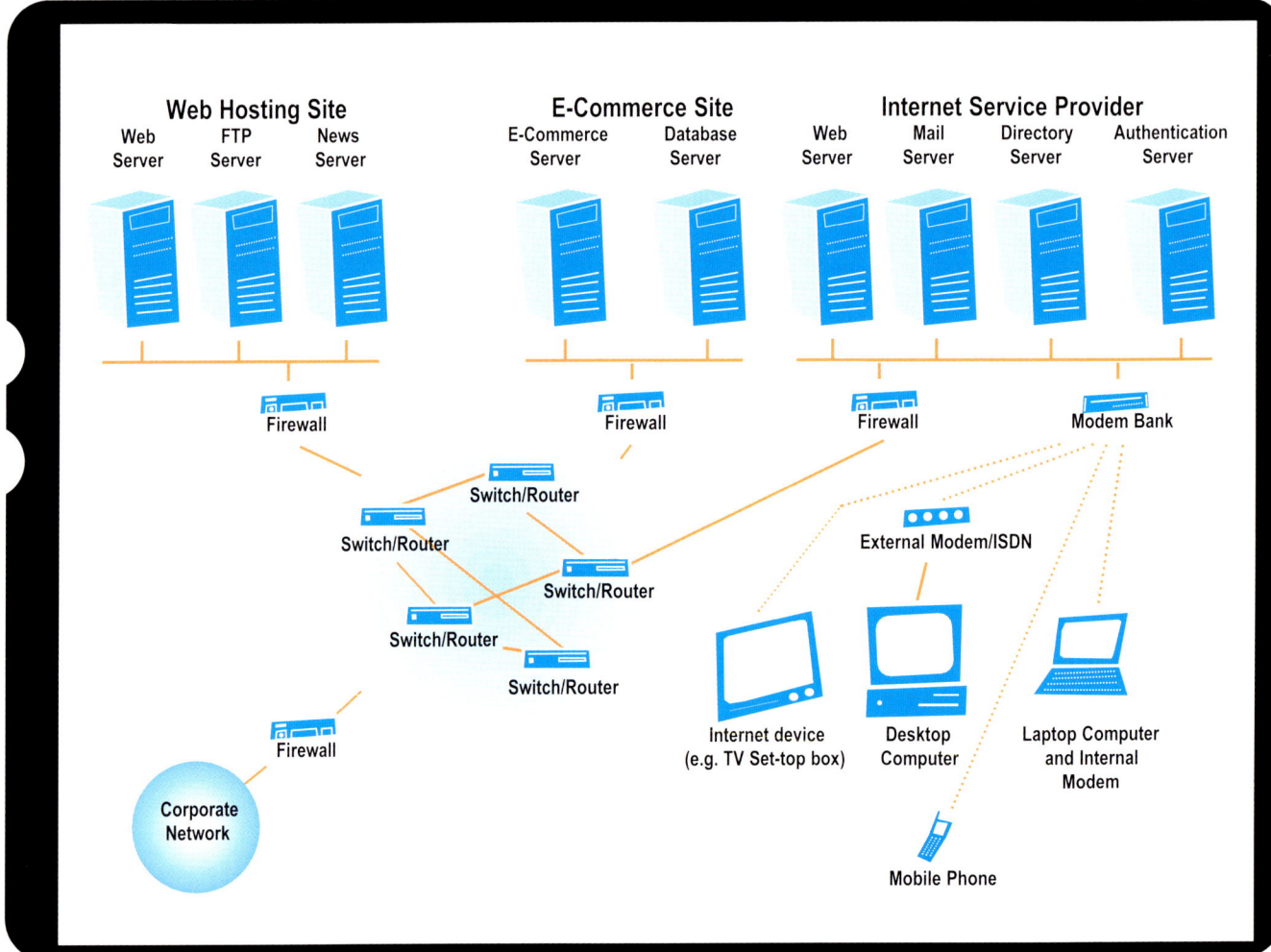

Buying software

Having sorted out the domain name and the web space, the charity then needs to buy some hardware and software to prepare the photographs, **graphics**, videos and **animations** that will form the basis of its web pages, and to test that they work properly.

The people

A team of people is needed to design and manage a large website. Typically, there is a project manager who oversees the project and makes sure that all the individuals in the team are working to schedule. The project manager works with two main groups of people – the **programmers** and the designers. The actual website will be put together by web programmers. These are people who are trained to use the various web editing software programmes. They understand **HTML** – the language used to write the web pages. The programmers may also be responsible for ensuring the security of the site. This is essential for preventing people from gaining unauthorized access to materials, and for **e-commerce**. The programmers can only put the web pages together once they have the content, including the text, graphics and other media that will be displayed on the web pages. The designers are responsible for the appearance of the website. The design team may include a graphic designer who produces the graphics for the site.

Many companies can offer web design services. They have design studios equipped with computers running design and web authoring programmes.

Hackers

Hackers are people who break through security systems to gain access to computers. Sometimes it is done for fun, sometimes for theft, and occasionally the damage is simply malicious. In early 2000, a hacker blackmailed an on-line music store by stealing and threatening to publish the credit card numbers of its customers. Also in 2000, a hacker crippled several major websites by overloading the sites with a barrage of messages. The hacker planted a malicious code on computers around the USA, and activated the programs remotely to bombard the target web servers with false messages, causing them to crash.

The tools of the trade

HyperText Markup Language (HTML) is a text mark up system used to produce web pages. It is basically a series of **tags** that control how the elements of a page are displayed. The file extension is *.html* or *.htm*. You can see the HTML code that is controlling the appearance and layout of a web page by looking at the HTML source. Most **browsers** allow you to view it, and you can clearly see the tags as they are contained within angle brackets <like this>. If the browser does not recognize a tag, it simply ignores it.

Web authoring software

In the early days of the Internet, **programmers** used to write their own HTML code. Nowadays, however, there are many different software packages designed to make life easier for the web programmer. The easiest way is to use a WYSIWYG (what you see is what you get) web page authoring program. It operates much like a word processing package and not only writes the HTML but also helps to put together the page. This program is especially useful for those who do not want to learn about HTML. Once people start programming in HTML on a production level, they often use HTML editing programs. These have special features that make HTML editing easier and faster.

There are also software packages to help produce **animations** on the web page. Animations are **graphics** that may blink, change shape, move or change colour. Complex animations can be written using a program called Macromedia ® Flash™. Animations, and other active elements such as forms, are often controlled by simple programs that are **downloaded** when a user opens a web page. The programs are called **applets** and they are written in a language called **Java**.

HTML is just a series of tags. The first lines of code refer to the title of the page and the associated key words. Further down you can see the tags controlling the colours used on the page, the size and alignment of a table and the type and size of the fonts.

```
<HTML>
<HEAD>
<META NAME="GENERATOR" Content="Microsoft Visual Studio 6.0">
</HEAD>
<BODY bgColor=#FFFFFF leftMargin=0 rightMargin=0 topMargin=0 marginwidth="0


<TABLE align=left bgColor=#cccccc border=0 cellPadding=0 cellSpacing=0 widt
  <TR>
    <TD valign="middle" height="18" width="1"> </TD>
    <TD valign="middle" height="18"><font face="arial, helvetica" size="2">
 <a HREF="http://www.bh.com/listing/uk/default.asp?country=United+Kingdom&m
    </font>
    </TD>
    <TD valign="middle" align="right" height="18"><font color="#FFFFFF" face
        <a href="http://www.bh.com/resellers" target=_top><font color="#fff
    </font>
    </TD>
  </TR>
</TABLE>

<br clear="all">


<TABLE align="left" bgColor=#ff0000 border=0 cellPadding=0 cellSpacing=0 wic


        <tr bgColor=#ff0000>
  <td> </td>
        <td align="right" width="35"><a href=http://www.bh.com/listing/uk/sub

  <td width="15%"><font face=Arial color=white size=2><B><a href=http://www

<!--     <td align="right" width="35"><img src="../images/navbar/account.gi

  <td width="15%"><font face="Arial" color="#ffffff" size="2"><B><a href=ht
-->
    <td align="right" width="35"><a href=http://www.bh.com/listing/uk/subinde

        <td width="15%"><font face="Arial" color="#ffffff" size="2"><B><a hre
```

Beyond HTML

HTML is a powerful tool for storing and exchanging small hypertext documents. However, it does have limitations, such as its fixed set of tags. A new language, XML or Extensible Markup Language, is being developed to work alongside HTML. XML lets programmers define their own set of tags and attributes. It complements HTML by enabling different kinds of **data** to be exchanged over the Web.

Web authoring software allows a web designer to build web pages on screen. It is easy to alter the size and colour of fonts and to position elements such as artwork and photographs.

On the job

Computer programmers write computer code, that is, they write the detailed instructions that tell the computer how to perform a certain function. They need a good knowledge of computer systems so will probably have taken a degree in computer science. A programmer needs mathematical skills and an ability to solve problems. He or she must be logical and pay attention to detail.

The site map

A lot of planning goes into designing a **website**. It is unwise to rush ahead and start designing pages without first considering the look and feel of the whole site. The arrangement of the different pages – where they are located and which are linked together – needs to be considered too. Some areas of the website may need to look different from others. For example, a children's area should have a different look from an adult-oriented news area.

The planning meeting

Early in the project, the web team gets together with representatives from the charity and discusses the content of the website. They need to agree on the design theme and the general **navigation** principles. They will probably consider the basic layout of the web pages and work on design issues such as the size of the screen and the position of the navigation bar. The key to a good design is simplicity – users should not have too many choices.

The web design team may present the client with a few alternative designs. Once a design is selected, the web team gets to work on the site navigation and the design of common features such as the appearance and position of buttons and the type, size and colour of the fonts.

Web styles

Websites generally fall into three common styles – hierarchical, linear and webbed. The hierarchical style is similar to an organizational chart where the **home page** has links to the most important pages, which have links to sub-categories and so on. However, it is important not to have too many levels. Visitors will tend to give up looking if too many sub-pages are offered before they find what they want.

The linear style is like a path through the website. Movement is limited to forwards and backwards along the designated path, so that the visitor sees all the pages in a specific order. No jumps to other areas of the site are provided, except for a return to the home page. A webbed style is perhaps the most haphazard, with most pages having many links to other pages on the site and many links leading off the site. Visitors can find this style of website confusing, and may get lost and leave it.

Many websites make use of frames. Frames control the way in which the web pages are displayed in the **browser's** window. The **HTML** instructs the browser to divide the window into several separate areas, and these are called frames. Normally, when you click on a **hyperlink**, the page containing the hyperlink is replaced by the page that the hyperlink points to. When a website uses frames, the page containing the hyperlink does not disappear. Instead, the new page is displayed in a separate frame. Usually, there is a frame containing all the hyperlinks so it acts as a navigation bar or a table of contents.

Planning for the future

It is almost impossible to anticipate all the different areas that might be needed in the future, so the design needs to be adaptable and able to expand to take in new areas or functions. The average size of the monitor is getting larger. A few years ago most people had 15 inch monitors, but now 17 inch is the norm. This affects the design of the page, as more information can be accommodated.

In the future, many people will access the Internet via TV screens and mobile phones. Designers of today's websites have to anticipate how their design will look on a TV screen, or even on the tiny screen of a mobile phone. TV screens do not display colours in the same way as a computer monitor. It is also impossible to scroll down on a TV screen, so many designers today are planning ahead by having non-scrolling web pages. Designing for a screen on a mobile phone presents even more problems since these users will want a quick **download** time and text that they can scroll through, rather than **graphics**.

Technical tips

When a group of people work on a website, they may produce web pages that differ slightly in appearance by, for example, using the wrong font or background colour. Cascading style sheets (CSS) avoid this problem. A style sheet is simply an HTML file that tells a browser how the page should appear on the screen. The file instructs the browser on the type, size and colour of font, the margins, layouts and so on. One style sheet can be linked to as many pages as necessary. When the designer makes any changes, only the style sheet needs to be modified, rather than every single page.

What is on the website?

Now the technical aspects of the project have been considered, it is important to plan the appearance and the features that will be displayed on the **website**.

First impressions

A shopper walking down a high street will often glance at a shop window, see if there is anything of interest, and quickly decide whether or not to go inside. The **home page** of a website is just like a shop window. It has to be eye-catching and interesting so that the visitor is tempted to venture further into the site. However, there has to be a balance between an interesting home page and one that is too cluttered and difficult to navigate. Ideally, there should be links from this page to the main areas of the site, often by use of a **navigation** bar that appears in the same place on each page.

Providing information

The charity's website needs to be able to carry out a wide range of activities. The main one is to provide information about its charitable work. It will want to display information about its work, perhaps giving a brief history, present its plans for the future and give details of how the visitors can make contact. The information needs to be presented in a lively but informative manner, with suitable **graphics**.
It may be necessary to have several areas, each focusing on one aspect of the charity's work. The charity may want to have a campaign area where they can tell the public about special projects that are under way and the various fund-raising activities that are being carried out.

News and views

The charity's press office will probably want to have an area devoted to press releases. This is where they will post their news for the media to see and report. There will probably be an archive area, which lists all the previous press releases in date order. There may even be an image archive.

Many charities publish a magazine or newsletter, and this too can be delivered **on-line**. The magazine section may have its own home page, which will highlight all the articles within a particular issue. There will be **hyperlinks** from the home page straight to the articles. The on-line magazine can be laid out in the same way as the paper version, or it could be given a different look and feel.

On the job

A press officer is responsible for writing the press releases that are sent to newspapers and magazines. Good written and oral communication skills are essential for this job. Press officers need to be able to put together press releases at short notice, write in an interesting but informative way and generate interest in their organization. They are usually the first point of contact for journalists and other interested parties who want to report on the activities of the organization.

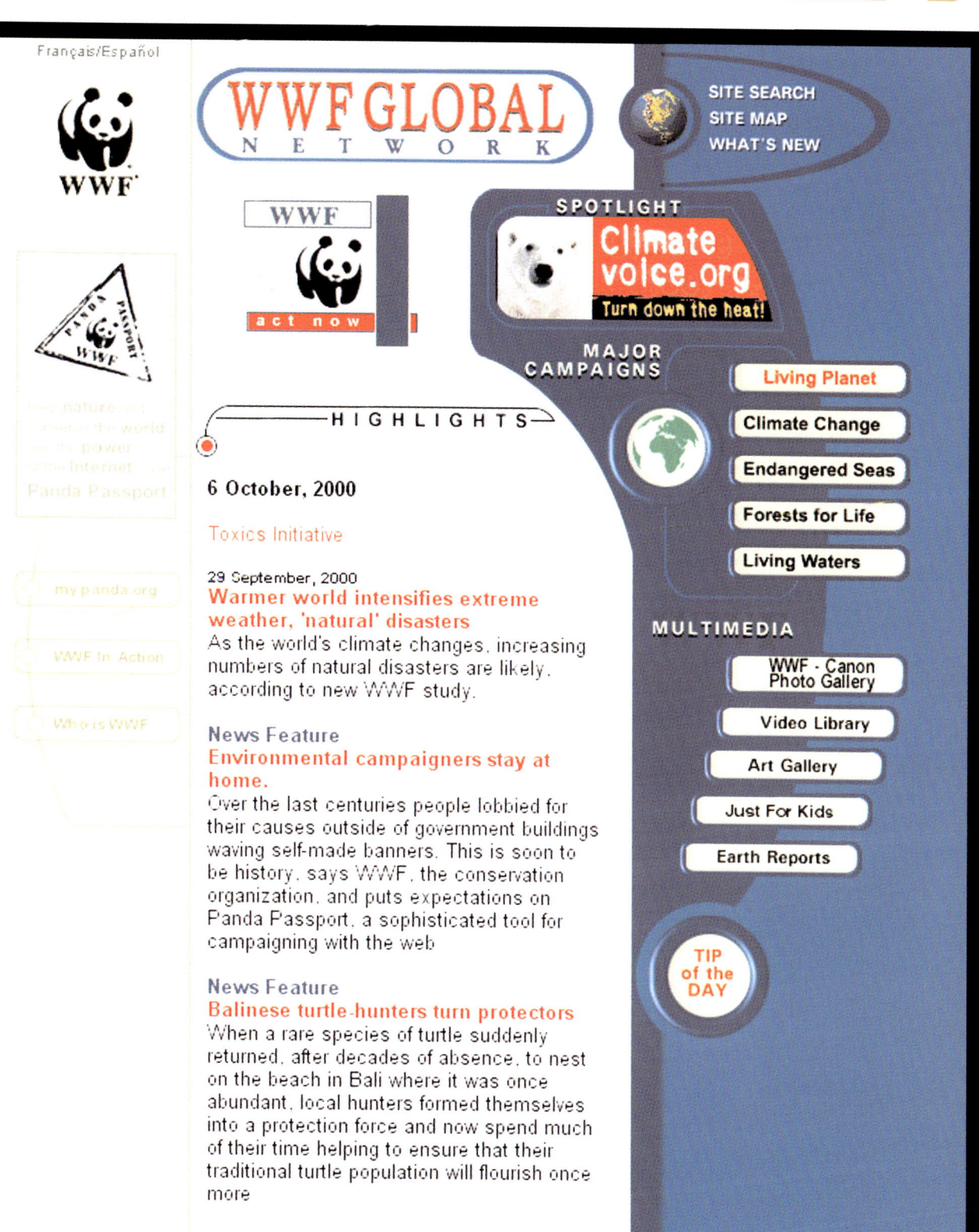

WWF GLOBAL
N E T W O R K

WWF

WWF

act now

SITE SEARCH
SITE MAP
WHAT'S NEW

SPOTLIGHT

Climate voice.org
Turn down the heat!

MAJOR CAMPAIGNS

Living Planet
Climate Change
Endangered Seas
Forests for Life
Living Waters

— H I G H L I G H T S —

6 October, 2000

Toxics Initiative

29 September, 2000
Warmer world intensifies extreme weather, 'natural' disasters
As the world's climate changes, increasing numbers of natural disasters are likely, according to new WWF study.

News Feature
Environmental campaigners stay at home.
Over the last centuries people lobbied for their causes outside of government buildings waving self-made banners. This is soon to be history, says WWF, the conservation organization, and puts expectations on Panda Passport, a sophisticated tool for campaigning with the web

News Feature
Balinese turtle-hunters turn protectors
When a rare species of turtle suddenly returned, after decades of absence, to nest on the beach in Bali where it was once abundant, local hunters formed themselves into a protection force and now spend much of their time helping to ensure that their traditional turtle population will flourish once more

my panda.org

WWF In Action

Who is WWF

MULTIMEDIA

WWF - Canon Photo Gallery

Video Library

Art Gallery

Just For Kids

Earth Reports

TIP of the DAY

appnet

Visitors to the website of the World Wide Fund for Nature have plenty to look at. They can find out about the charity's major campaigns, read the news headlines, visit the children's pages, wander through the photo and art galleries or become a member.

Commercial activities on the website

As well as providing information to the public, the **website** will also be used as a means of generating income for the charity. This can be done in several ways.

Joining up new members

Many charities rely on their membership for the bulk of their income, so it is important that visitors are given an opportunity to join the charity. Charities that carry out their work around the world may want to set up web pages in different languages, such as French or Spanish, to maximize their membership. Visitors are prompted to choose a language when they first visit the site, and they are automatically directed by **hyperlink** to the web pages displaying the chosen language.

The membership area on the site will need to list all the benefits of joining the charity, as well as the costs. It is important to give visitors the chance to join **on-line**, for if they have enjoyed their visit, or become motivated by the content, they can join straight away, as a spur of the moment thing. Ideally, they will be able to complete an on-line form and pay their membership by credit card. This means that the membership area of the site has to be secure and handle **e-commerce** transactions.

This barn owl has been starring on BBC Nature Online. A webcam (left) was placed behind its nest box so that visitors to the Web could watch the barn owl raise its young. Some sites require visitors to subscribe before viewing webcam images.

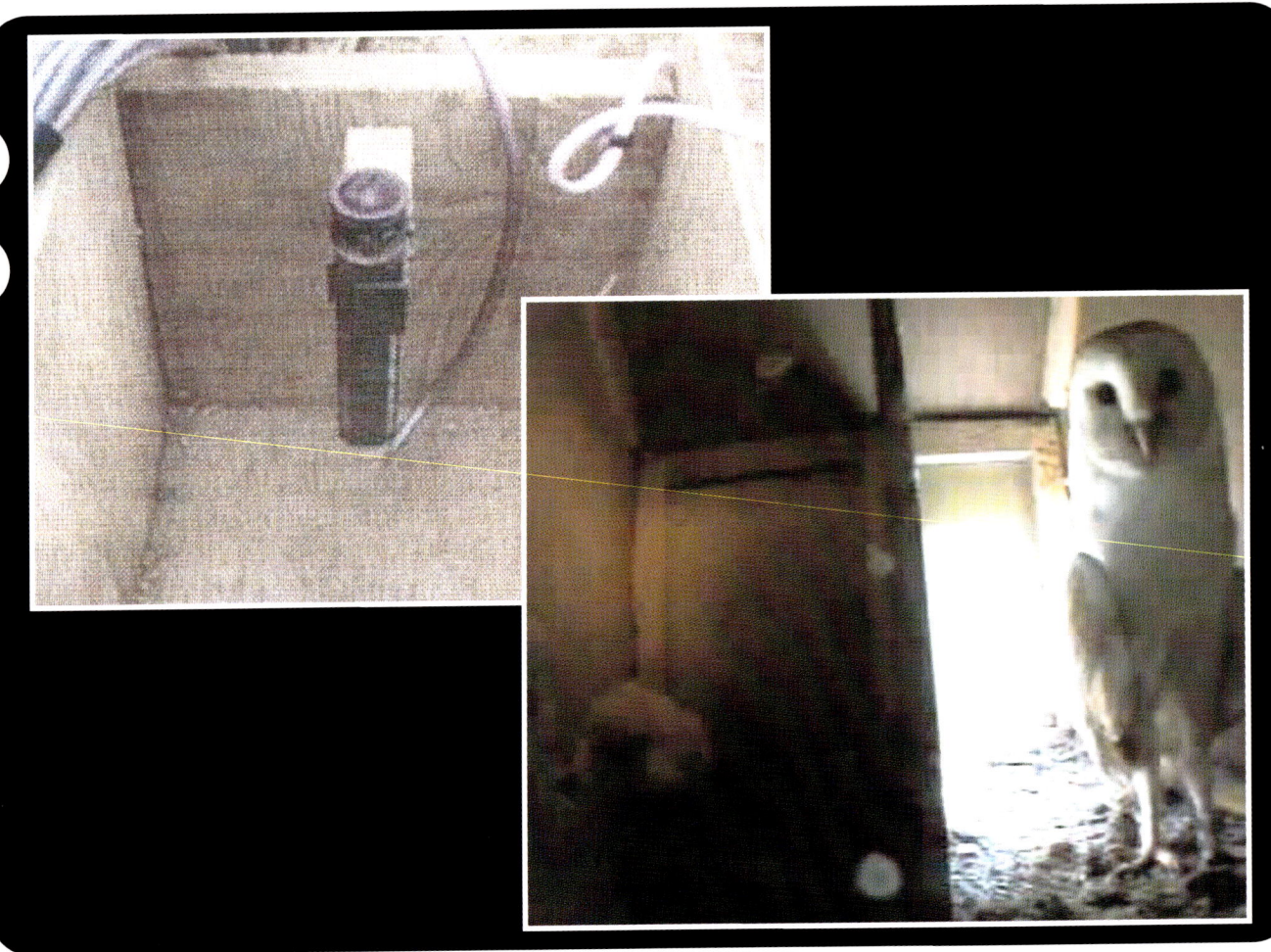

Selling gifts

Charities usually sell gift items like greetings cards, wrapping paper, tea towels, sweatshirts, T-shirts and toys to raise money. All of these items can be displayed in the on-line shop, where e-commerce programs allow the visitor to put the items in their 'shopping trolley' at a click of the mouse. They have to be able to pay by credit, and their credit card details must be transmitted safely to the computer, without any fear of interruption or eavesdropping. To do this, the payment is usually handled by a special secure site that **encrypts** the information flowing between the **browser** and the web **server**. Browsers indicate that the communications are secure by means of a small **icon**, such as a padlock, at the bottom of the screen.

Exchanging information

Members and visitors alike will probably have the same interests and want to talk to a member of staff or to each other. All this is possible on a modern website, which can provide a chat room where visitors and staff can 'talk' to each other by typing messages. It is also possible to set up on-line conferences and forums on particular topics. Electronic bulletin boards announce details of when specific conferences will be held. Staff members can even have their own web pages with **e-mail** links so that visitors can write directly to them.

In the past, charities sold most of their gift items through mail order catalogues or from stalls at fairs and other events. Now, visitors to their website can buy the goods direct using their credit cards.

Putting the Site Together

Building the site

The preparation of a **website** involves skills that may not be called upon again. So companies often put together a project team whose job is to build and publish the website, or the job is sometimes handed to a specialist web development company. The day-to-day management and maintenance of the completed site is then carried out by a different group of people.

Project management

A project is an activity that brings together people with different skills and resources to achieve a specified aim, in this case to build a fully functional website. Most projects have to be completed within a specified period of time and have a given budget. The first person to be appointed is usually the project manager, who will decide on his or her team and put together a schedule. The project is first broken down into tasks, which are placed in sequence and the estimated time for completion of each is calculated.

Programmers are responsible for building the website, compiling the different pages and checking that everything works properly. Although they can start work early in the project, especially in getting the basic layout prepared, they need the visual content from the rest of the team in order to start serious work on the site.

The visual content

Graphic designers are responsible for the graphics on the pages. Very often, a web page is built from lots of tiny graphics, laid down carefully to build up the whole screen. The designers use image manipulation programs such as Adobe Photoshop ® and Illustrator ® to make the buttons, **navigation** bars, and **home page** graphics.

The text on the website needs to be written too. The web author of the team writes the screen text and defines the **hyperlinks** to connect it to different parts of the website. Often the text has to be relatively short, so that it fits the screen. Editors check the text and graphics on the screen, making sure that they work together, that their position is correct and that all hyperlinks work properly.

On the job

Project managers need a number of different skills. Obviously, they need certain technical skills so that they can understand the project and the tasks that are involved. But, more importantly, they have to be able to lead and motivate a group of people who come from a range of backgrounds, so good interpersonal skills and business experience are essential. The project manager's job is demanding and varied, including planning and staffing the project, monitoring progress, reviewing work and adjusting schedules where necessary, controlling the budget and carrying out performance tests.

A project manager does not need to be an expert in all areas of web design, but he or she will be expected to know enough, so that they can understand what each member of the team is doing.

Web content

The pages of the charity's **website** need content. Some of this will come from the archives of the charity, such as past editions of magazines and newsletters. However, the content for a web page is often written from scratch, because the audience, the page size and the format are different.

*Once a photograph is taken and the film developed, the photographs can be **scanned** and placed on a web page. **Digital** cameras, like the one being used here, allow photographers to download the photographs from the camera straight on to the computer.*

Words and pictures

Journalists and photographers can be paid to produce content for the website. Their words and photographs can be posted on the site, and additional images can be bought from photo libraries. There are a number of **on-line** photo libraries where visitors can log on and search through the library's **database** to find images. These on-line libraries allow people to place images in their 'shopping basket'. Then, low-**resolution** images can be **downloaded** and viewed on the web page. If the image looks right, a licence to use it can be bought from the photo library. Photographic licences usually specify the size and, perhaps, the period for which the image can be displayed. Video clips can be bought from film libraries in much the same way.

Checking for accuracy

It is very easy to put together a web page quickly and post it on a website. Sometimes, the process occurs so quickly that few people have time to check the content for accuracy. A printed publication is much more permanent, and may go through several checks – by editors and proof-readers – to make sure that there are no mistakes before it is printed. Because they can be changed so easily, web pages are often posted without these checks. Potentially, millions of people could read the web page and use the information found upon it, so it is very important to get it absolutely correct. It is also very important to check that the information is not libellous, for example. Libel – the injuring of a person's reputation by making false statements about them – applies to web pages just as much as it does to words printed in newspapers and books.

Copyright issues

People also have to be very careful that they have permission to publish the information that they post on their web pages. Words and images cannot just be copied from anywhere, because they are protected by copyright. The person who created the words or images is the copyright holder. Anybody wishing to use other people's words and photographs on their web pages has to have the copyright holder's permission. So the wildlife charity needs to check that it holds the copyright to the material that it publishes on the Web, or that it has obtained the correct permission from the copyright holders.

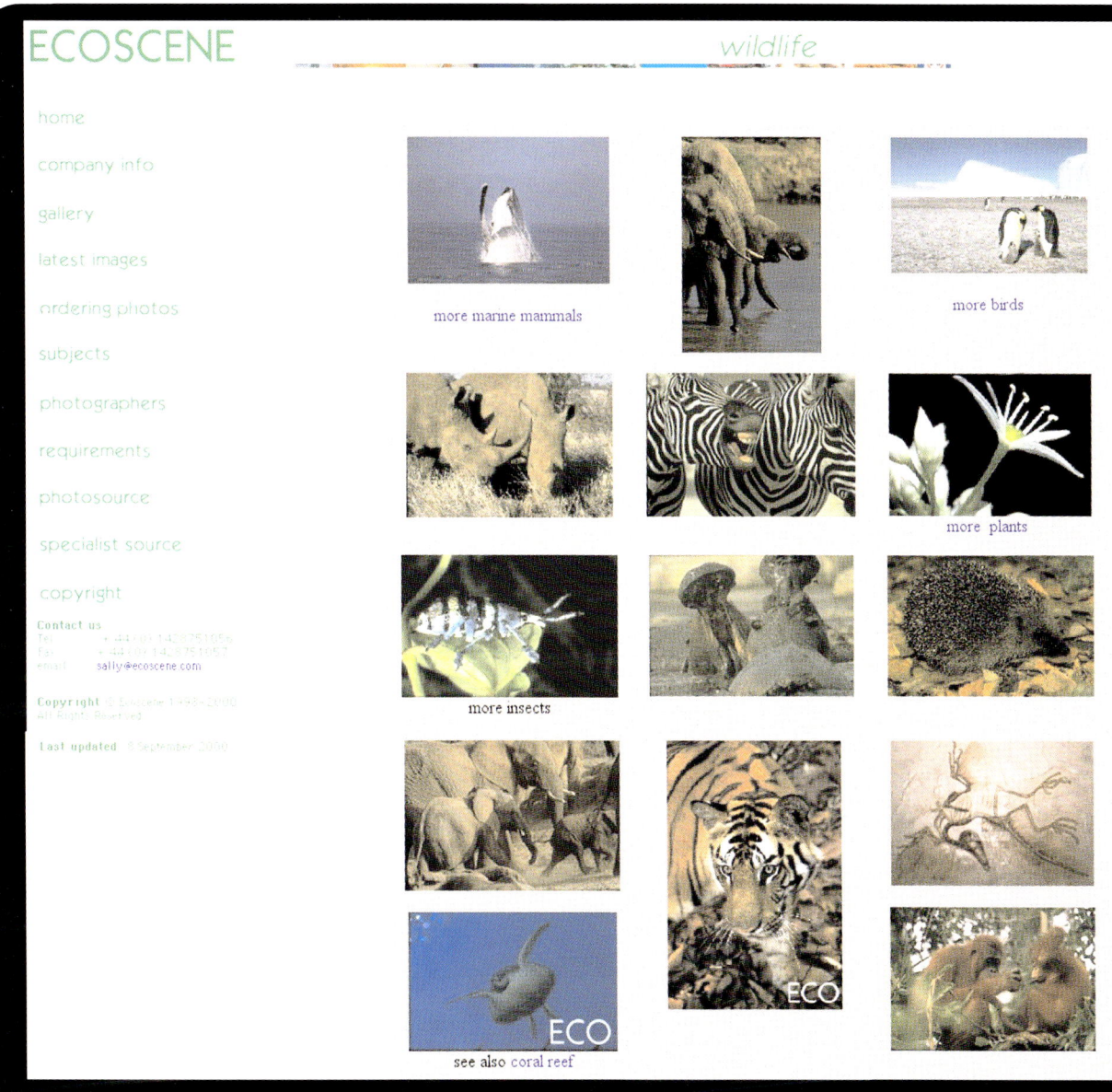

Sometimes, the images and information displayed on websites are copyright-free. However, this website displays photographs which are all protected by copyright, and the visitor cannot use the images without seeking permission first.

Putting together a web page

A typical web page usually consists of a heading and some body text, together with visual elements such as photographs, **graphics**, **animations** or videos. These elements all have to be carefully placed in the web page.

Static versus dynamic

Static pages are relatively straightforward to build, but they are not particularly interesting as the content does not change. A dynamic page is one that can be **interactive**. There are many degrees of interactivity. Simple scripting, such as a 'mouse-over' command that is activated when the mouse passes over a particular area, may send a message to the **browser** to swap images. Forms offer interaction by allowing the visitor to send specific information to the **website**. Perhaps the most sophisticated form of interaction is when the actual contents of the web page are derived from a **database**. This sort of complex interaction is usually a feature of search sites and **e-commerce** sites.

These schoolchildren are using flat bed scanners to convert photographs and artwork into digital images, for inclusion on a website.

Preparing the text

The text can either be written directly into the web pages using a web authoring tool, or it can be prepared in a word processing package and exported in **HTML** format. This is then imported into the web page and formatted. Any **hyperlinks** from the text can then be created.

Capturing images

Many journalists now use **digital** cameras because they are easy to use and there is no need to process film; the pictures can be sent straight back to the newspaper over a phone line using a computer with a **modem**. The quality of such an image is fine for web pages and newspapers, but it may not be good enough for magazine or book publishing. Photographs that already exist, in either print or transparency form, have to be **scanned** to produce a digital image. Then, the images have to be prepared for the web page, by reducing their **resolution** and altering their size. When you look at a photograph on a printed page you are looking at a high quality image. There are at least 300 dots of ink in every square inch of paper – the resolution is 300 dots per inch (dpi). The equivalent number of dots – or pixels – on a computer screen is just 72 dpi. So the image resolution has to be reduced from 300 dpi or more to just 72 dpi. Then the image is ready to be saved.

Graphic designers can edit web graphics while they are on the screen so they can see the effect of their changes straight away.

Images take up a lot of disk space, so they are usually **compressed** (made smaller) by converting them to **JPEG** format. This is a file type that compresses the digital information so that a screen size image can be **downloaded** in just a few seconds. Many photographic programs can compress the image for web display, so that there is a balance between image quality and the time taken to download it.

A **graphic** designer is responsible for producing the visual content of the website. He or she makes use of software packages such as Photoshop ® and Illustrator ® to create the designs on a computer. The computer makes the job much easier as graphics can be created more quickly with on-screen editing. The increase in demand for graphics for web pages means that graphic designers have to work in 3-D as well as 2-D.

On the job

As well as designing multimedia products and websites, graphic designers also work on the design and layout of magazines, newspapers and other printed publications. Most graphic designers take a course in design or visual communications. But more important than a certificate or degree is a good portfolio of work to show to prospective clients. Obviously, a graphic designer needs to have a flair for design, but just as important is the ability to interpret the wishes of the client, rather than to impose any personal preferences.

Moving images

More **websites** are now using video as a means of attracting attention. Technological developments in **compression** and **decompression**, and faster communications with the Internet, mean that **programmers** can now integrate video into a web page. Video can be **downloaded** for playback later but, if communications are good enough, video can also be 'streamed'. This means that the video can be decompressed and played back in **real-time**, as it is received. Streaming video is attractive because, even though it is of much lower quality, there is hardly any wait before playback begins. Video usually has an audio soundtrack, which is also decompressed for playback.

Many websites linked to film or TV programmes use video, running short clips as a form of advertisement. Some TV programmes, such as the UK's 'Big Brother', rely on video cameras (known as webcams) to attract a huge audience. Visitors to the Big Brother website could watch real-time video recordings from any of the 24 cameras placed around the Big Brother house. On this site, there was a three-minute delay to allow the producers of the programme to carry out any necessary editing.

Webcams can also be placed in interesting locations such as nest sites, water holes or even coral reefs, providing valuable information for scientists as well as fascinating viewing for website visitors.

Video editing

Although it is time-consuming, the process of **digitizing**, editing, and **uploading** video files is not a particularly complicated process. The key question to ask is 'What value does the video add to the website?'. The benefit must justify the effort spent digitizing the video and making it ready for the web page. At 28.8 **Kbps** (kilobytes per second), a 1-megabyte file representing just a few seconds of video can take about ten minutes to download. Many visitors to the website will not want to spend so much time downloading.

Animations

Animators create moving **graphics** using specialist software packages. An **animation** can be a simple series of images, which are displayed one after another. Each image is called a frame. The time delay between each frame and the number of times the animation is played can be set by the software. 3-D animations are far more complex. First, the animator builds a mesh or wire-frame to which they apply surface colours and textures. Then they set the movement of the object and the viewpoints of cameras. Once the animator is satisfied with the appearance and movement, the whole animation is carried out frame by frame.

Technical tips

There are three main video file types that are found on the **Web**: QuickTime, AVI and MPEG. AVI is an older format with relatively little compression. MPEG and QuickTime are most commonly found, with QuickTime probably being the most popular – many large entertainment sites use QuickTime exclusively.

*Animations can make an otherwise dull screen look interesting. However, the user does have to have a recent version of their **browser** installed which can cope with playing back animations.*

E-commerce

Most people think that electronic commerce, or **e-commerce**, simply means **on-line** shopping. But shopping is only a small part of e-commerce. It now includes on-line banking, **real-time** share trading and business-to-business commercial transactions. In addition, there are growing systems for so-called micro-transactions, which let people pay tiny amounts of money, often just a few pence, to access on-line content. In fact, e-commerce refers to all the systems that let money change hands over the Internet.

On-line bookshops allow the visitor to search for a particular book title, author or publisher of a book. Often, reviews of the chosen titles are displayed. As well as searching for a title, a visitor can browse the books listed under different subjects, just like wandering around a bookshop.

Shopping on the Web

On-line shopping is very straightforward. The **website** displays the items that are for sale, together with the price. If the shopper wishes to buy the item, they simply click on it and it is placed in their electronic 'shopping trolley'. The shopper can place as many items as they like in the shopping trolley, and remove any if they wish. The screen displays the total cost of the items, any taxes and the shipping charge. Then the shopper is taken to a secure area where he or she can complete an on-line form with their credit card details. In the secure area, web pages let the **server** and the **browser** swap information that **encrypts** and **decrypts** the information flowing between them. Anyone intercepting the communications would not be able to understand the scrambled information.

Credit is essential

Ownership of a credit card is essential to current e-commerce. However, many computer users are too young to own a credit card but keen to pay for things on-line, especially to obtain music and play on-line games. Several systems are being developed to provide 'electronic wallets', including secure, refillable, electronic money tokens.

Security

Credit card users are usually protected against fraud by their credit card companies – and it is often the retailer who is liable for any loss. While e-commerce companies set up secure communications to protect transmitted information, the **data** is still vulnerable when stored in a computer. Secure storage of information is a critical element of any modern website. Far too many companies store credit card and other personal data in simple text files, and then fail to protect their systems from **hackers**.

In the UK, users of the Internet are protected by the Data Protection Act. Companies trading on the Internet, and who keep data about their visitors, are required to register with the Data Protection Registrar and must agree only to use the data in certain ways.

Websites with e-commerce sections let the visitor know when they are entering a secure part of the site. There is usually a small symbol which looks like a padlock at the bottom of the web page.

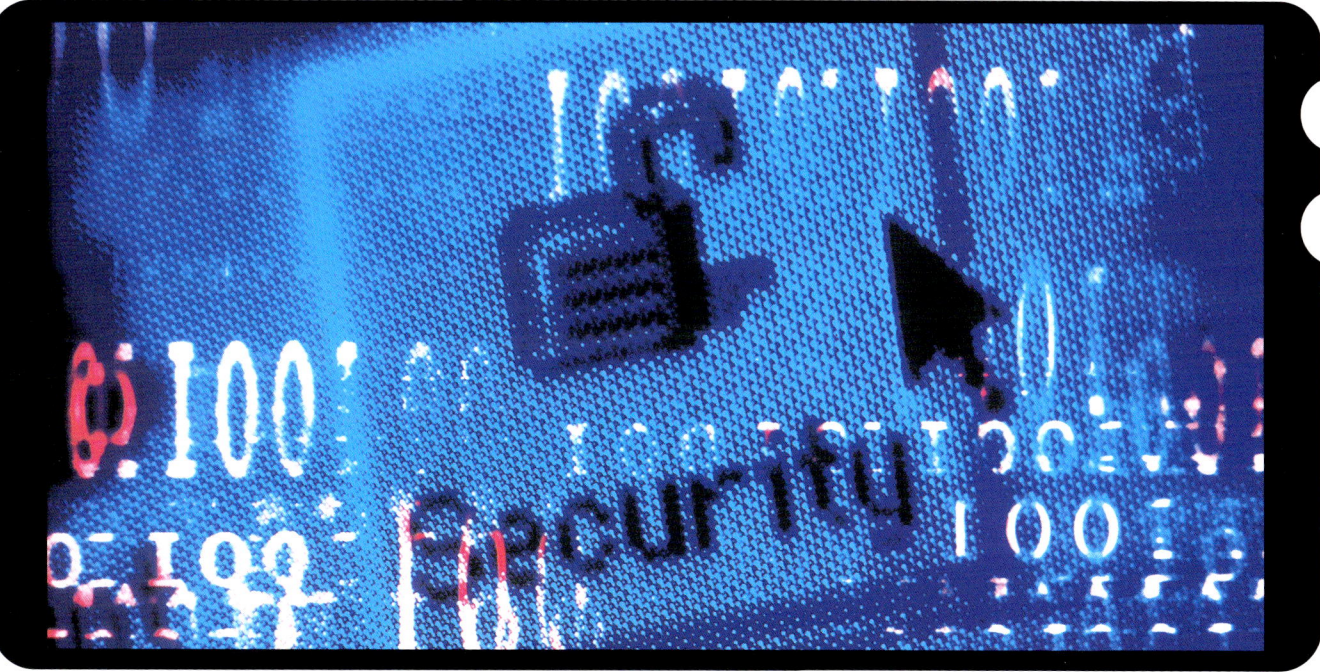

Technical tips

When a computer, or a network of computers in a business, is linked to the Internet, special security measures are required to prevent unauthorized access. A **firewall** is a piece of software or hardware that prevents unauthorized communication into and out of the computer or internal network. The organization that owns the computer or the network can then enforce a security policy on traffic flowing between its network and the Internet.

Chat rooms

An Internet chat room can be described as a 'virtual party'. With web chat, people can communicate in **real-time** with other people all around the world. In most cases, users do not need any special software, just their web **browser**. Actually, the word 'chat' is somewhat misleading, because it does not really involve talking to anyone, just typing and reading text messages that have been written by other people in the 'virtual room'. Once a visitor enters a chat room, which could be a web page that runs special software, they can choose just to read the exchanges (which is known as 'lurking') or they can join in by posting their own messages.

Chatting

Most chat rooms require the visitor to register. Real names can be used, but many people prefer to make up a name. Not only does this conceal their identity, offering them some privacy, but it lets them assume a new identity. It is similar to role playing, where a visitor can be anyone they want.

Once the visitor has chosen their chat 'persona', they may also be able to select an image to represent themselves. These **graphics**, known as 'avatars', can be anything from a frog to a princess. Although communicating **on-line** lacks the nuances of talking face-to-face, these friendly graphics can personalize the experience in a small way, and break the monotony of a text-only screen. Once equipped with a name and possibly an avatar, the visitor follows the instructions to choose a room and clicks on the enter button. Once inside, the visitor will probably find themselves in the middle of a conversation. They are wise to 'lurk' for a few minutes to get the gist of the exchange, before joining in. As the interaction continues, new postings appear at the top or bottom of the list.

One of the most important rules of chat rooms is never to give out personal information to any stranger you meet on-line, especially not your address, phone number, credit card number, school address or photograph. You should avoid private conversations. There have been incidents in which individuals have used the Internet to contact young people with the intent of harming them.

Being safe on-line

It is essential to take certain safety precautions when chatting on-line:

- ✿ Never respond on-line to any messages that use words that are bad, scary, threatening, or just feel weird
- ✿ If you get that kind of a message, print it out or make a copy, and tell an adult immediately
- ✿ If you have been harassed or had trouble on-line, you should contact your **ISP** immediately
- ✿ Never arrange a private face-to-face meeting with someone you have met on-line
- ✿ If you do decide to meet a 'cyberpal', make sure you meet in a public place and that a parent or other adult is with you.

Chat hosts

Many chat rooms employ chat hosts. Chat hosts are usually trained volunteers who help to make the chat room a more friendly place. They usually work two-hour shifts several times a week. A typical chat host is a friendly, courteous person who is available to people who visit the chat room. They assist and educate members and handle difficult situations. Some chat hosts are employed to police the chat room by monitoring the chat. They have the authority to remove members who use bad language or who threaten other members. Chat hosts are particularly important in chat rooms that are visited by young people.

Many websites have a chat room. Often, well known people such as actors, TV personalities and musicians are invited to a chat room at a particular time to 'chat' with members of the public. Chatting is a good way to exchange ideas with like-minded people. However, visitors to chat rooms have to remember that they have no way of checking the identity of the people with whom they are 'talking'.

Features versus speed

The design team has to agree on the look and feel of the **website**, but there are other issues to consider, especially **usability download** times, and how it will look on different types of computer.

Download time

Downloading some pages can take a long time, especially those featuring large photographs. People can get bored waiting for the photograph to appear and move on to another web page.

Large **graphics** or photographs on a web page may look very attractive, but, the bigger they are, the longer they take to download. If people get bored waiting for the images to appear, they may move on to another page, so it is often better to have a smaller version of the photograph, known as a 'thumbnail' because of its size, which downloads in a few seconds. The thumbnail is linked to the larger photograph so that, if anybody wishes to see more detail, they can click on the thumbnail to load the larger photograph. This larger image could even have additional features, such as a 'zoomable' area, but such features are best restricted to the second page, since the first page needs to have a fast download time and should not be cluttered.

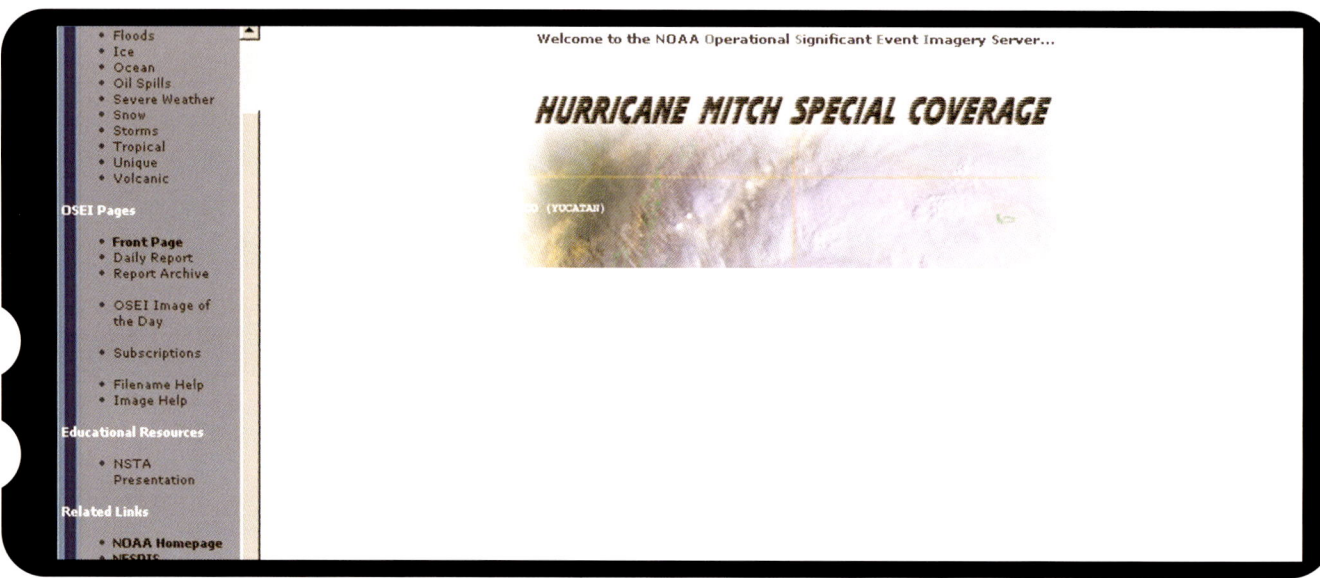

Apple Mac or PC?

It is important to look at the web pages on different computers, since web pages look slightly different when viewed, for example, on a PC compared with an Apple Mac. The visual elements produced on a Mac can look too dark on a PC, while those compiled on the PC often look washed-out on a Mac screen. Another factor is the size of the screen. The two most common **resolutions** are 640 x 480 and 800 x 600, while many people now use 1024 x 768. The fact is, it is very difficult to make pages visually appealing at all resolutions. Instead of trying to make the pages look great at one resolution at the expense of another, it is often better to settle for making the pages look good at both common resolutions. This involves a little extra fine-tuning and fiddling, but the results are worth it.

Not all the visitors will be using a personal computer. Some people may use web TV, which has only 625 lines of resolution (in the UK), cannot scroll up and down nor show some colours properly.

Testing the site

Testing is an essential phase in the project. One approach is to ask people who are not involved with the design to test-run the site. People do things in odd and unexpected ways, so even the most carefully-planned project will learn from usability testing how user-friendly it is. Also, the testers will click on all the **hyperlinks** to make sure they are working and that all the visual elements are in the right place. They may discover dead-end pages that will not let the visitor escape without being forced to use their **browser's navigation** system. It is important to make sure that all images load correctly and that they have alternate text for those who have elected to turn off graphics or are using browsers incapable of showing graphics. Checks need to be made on any forms to make sure they work properly.

Browser differences

HTML can be interpretted slightly differently by different browsers, or even by different versions of the same browser. The HTML author can fix some features, such as the relative size of the headings and the space between the blocks of text, but the user can adjust other features. For example, the size of the standard font, the size of the window, and the resolution at which the page is viewed will all affect the appearance of the screen. A carefully laid out table may look great on one computer, but under different conditions can look totally different. It is therefore very important to check the website on the most popular browsers, Internet Explorer® and Netscape® Navigator, and to check if the pages look all right on older versions of each browser.

By simply changing the preferences in the browser, a user can alter the appearance of a web page. The web page at the top has a relatively small font. It looks very different when viewed using a larger font and different typeface (bottom).

Going Live

Getting visitors

The charity's work does not stop once the **website** is up and running. Now it is time to start attracting visitors to the site. A few visitors may stumble across the website by chance, but the majority will only visit once they have been told of the site's address. The charity will want to place their web address on all their headed paper and advertise the site in their newsletters and magazines.

The role of search engines

How do members of the public find the website? They will probably find it by using a search engine, which is a system designed to locate and catalogue web pages. For example, a student is writing an essay on tigers and she wants to learn more about tiger behaviour. By using a search engine, such as Yahoo®, Google™ or AltaVista®, she can find suitable sites. She types in the key words she wants to search on, such as 'tiger' and 'endangered', and the search engine comes up with a list of relevant web pages. Quite often, the search returns hundreds of different pages, so it may have to be refined by adding more words. Yahoo® is slightly different from the others mentioned. It was once a straightforward search engine, but has expanded to become a 'portal' site, with links to categorized and reviewed sites, chat, webmail, news, jobs and auctions. There are both UK and US versions.

Although search engines do search and categorize the Web automatically, it is best to register the website with the main ones. Although there are literally hundreds of different search engines altogether, there are fewer than ten major ones. To register the site, the charity has to complete a form found on each search engine site, though there are free programs available that will automatically register a site with all the major search engines in one go.

Links

The charity can set up links that take visitors to other interesting sites. In the same way, other websites can provide return links. The wildlife charity may want links with other charities doing similar work, or to sites with interesting articles on issues that affect wildlife.

Technical tips

Search engines seek out web pages using smart programs called web crawlers and robots. Web crawlers and robots prowl the **Web** looking for documents and their web addresses. They collect this information and send it to the search engine's indexing software. The indexing software extracts information from the documents and stores it in a **database**. When a search is performed by a user entering key words, the database is searched for documents that match. The search engine assembles a web page that lists the results as hypertext links.

Unwelcome visitors

Viruses, worms and Trojan horses are software programs created specifically to wreak havoc on computers. Sometimes a strange message may appear on your screen. The worst that can happen is that all the **data** on your hard drive is wiped out and the computer itself is damaged. Malicious viruses can do thousands of pounds worth of damage in a very short time, disrupting businesses and threatening security.

These destructive programs exploit weaknesses in software to reproduce themselves and send copies to other computers around the world. If you **download** and run software from the Internet, or even receive **e-mail** attachments, there is a strong chance of picking up a virus. People can protect their computer by installing virus protection programs that scan the hard drive and downloaded files for viruses, deleting any they find.

A simple search on the words 'tiger' and 'endangered' revealed more than 42,000 different pages on this search engine. This search could be narrowed by adding further words such as 'poaching' or 'India'.

Advanced Search   Language, Display, & Filtering Options   Search Tips

tiger+endangered   [Google Search] [I'm Feeling Lucky]

Tip: in most browsers you can just hit the return key instead of clicking on the search button.

Google results 1-10 of about 42,000 for tiger+endangered. Search took 0.11 seconds.

Category: Society > Issues > Environment > Conservation and Endangered Species

Siberian Tiger -- Endangered Species
...areas of 1200-1600 square miles. **ENDANGERED**: It is estimated that there...
...Russia nearly 150-250. The Siberian **Tiger**. "The Great Wanderers", hunting...
www.greatcatsoftheworld.com/siberian.html - 9k - Cached - Similar pages

ENN News - Year of the Tiger focuses on animal's endangered
...Archive Year of the **Tiger** focuses on animal's **endangered** status...
...report found a 95 percent decline in **tiger** numbers over the last 100...
www.enn.com/enn-news-archive/1998/01/012898/tiger.asp - 26k - Cached - Similar pages

Bengal Tiger - African Endangered Species - WildLife Creations
...**Endangered** Gifts of Nature **Endangered** Bengal **Tiger** Photo...
...and Indo-Chinese - are listed as **endangered** on the U.S. **Endangered**...
wildlife-creations.com/animals/Bengal-Tiger-pic.htm - 6k - Cached - Similar pages

THE ENDANGERED TIGER
...THE **ENDANGERED TIGER** Tigers are among the most **endangered**...
...and a fourth, the South China **tiger**, is down to twenty animals. Recently....
www.lam.mus.ca.us/cats/P18/ - 4k - Cached - Similar pages

Tiger, tigers, tiger, big cats, endangered wildlife
...conservation of tigers and other **endangered** species. **Tiger** Facts...
...Common Name: **Tiger** Scientific Name: Panthera Tigris Weight: 200-500...
www.enteract.com/~eaglegb/indexpcs/tiger.html - 9k - Cached - Similar pages

Tiger (Endangered Species), Wildlife Species Information: U.S.
...critically **endangered** wildlife. In addition, all **tiger** species are...
...under the **Endangered** Species Act, prohibiting **tiger** parts and...
species.fws.gov/bio_tige.html - 9k - Cached - Similar pages

Committee on Resources: News Release (01/28/98) Endangered
...Reporter January 28, 1998 **Endangered Tiger** Rhinoceros Protection...
...assist conservation programs for **endangered** tigers and rhinoceros - two...
resourcescommittee.house.gov/press/1998/980128pr.htm - 10k - Cached - Similar pages

THE CRITICALLY ENDANGERED TIGER
...Very Poor THE CRITICALLY **ENDANGERED TIGER** by Judi Chapman August...
...exaggeration to say that the **tiger** is a critically **endangered**...
www.themestream.com/articles/113013.html - 21k - Cached - Similar pages

SchoolWorld Endangered Species Project: Tasmanian Tiger
...Internet Education Project **Endangered**/Threatened Species Report Submitted...
...Redcliffe, Queensland, Australia Tasmanian **Tiger** Tasmanian **Tiger**...
www.schoolworld.asn.au/species/tastiger.html - 5k - Cached - Similar pages

Tracking success

Awebsite needs constant review, and it is important to check on the numbers of visitors coming to the site. The web design needs fine-tuning and the content needs to be continually updated so that people make repeat visits.

Visitor numbers

The number of visitors to the site is a good indicator of how successful the site has been. So how does the charity know if people are visiting its site? One way to track the number of visitors is to place a simple counter on the **home page** that increases by one every time somebody **downloads** that page. However, a more accurate way is to analyse the log files generated by the web **server**, which records every time a page or page element is downloaded. There are now programs that will carry out a simple analysis to discover which are the most popular pages, which ones never get downloaded, the route through the website taken by users, the length of time they spent on the site and, sometimes, the continent from which they were visiting.

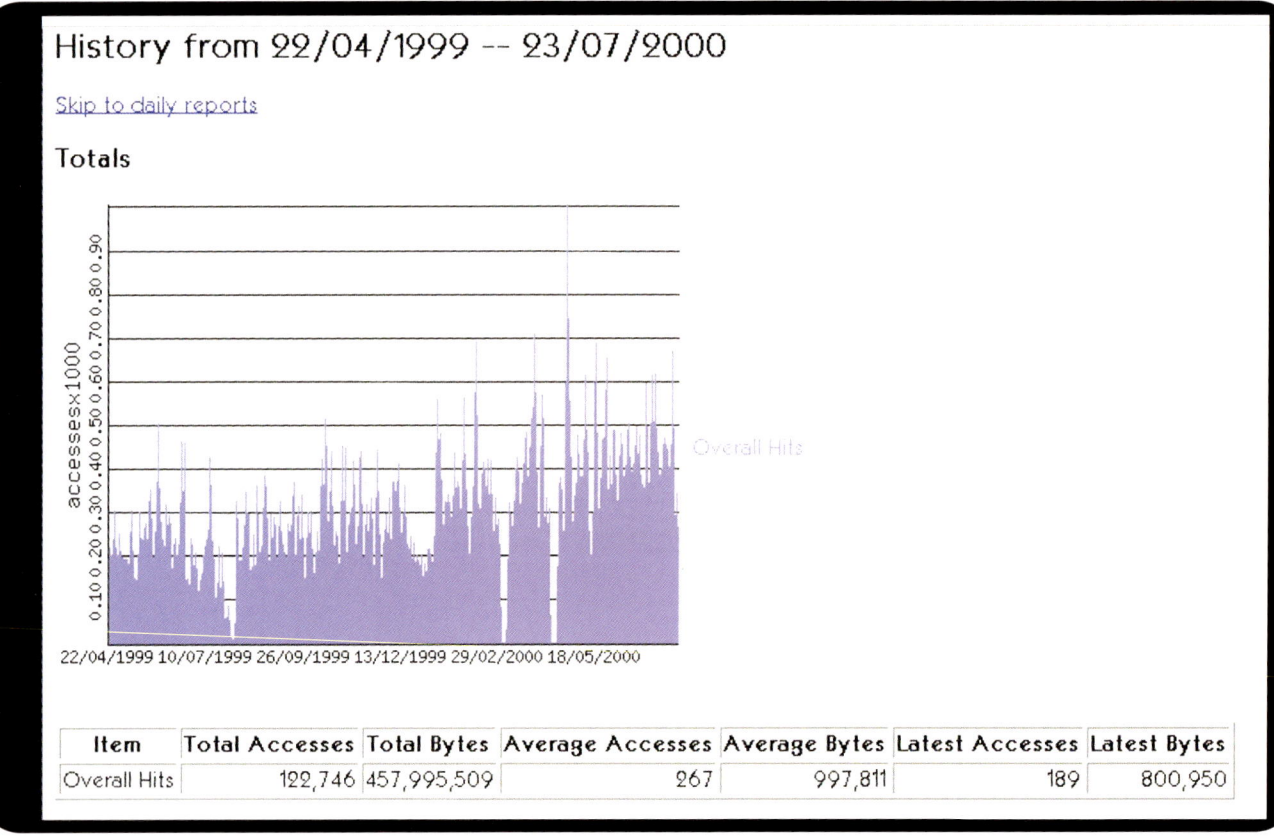

History from 22/04/1999 -- 23/07/2000

Skip to daily reports

Totals

Item	Total Accesses	Total Bytes	Average Accesses	Average Bytes	Latest Accesses	Latest Bytes
Overall Hits	122,746	457,995,509	267	997,811	189	800,950

The web logs in this picture show that this particular web page was accessed 122,746 times over a fifteen-month period, with an average of 267 accesses per day.

Registering the visitors

Some websites ask visitors to register before they can enter certain parts of the site. Each visitor is required to complete a form that asks for their name, postal address and **e-mail** address. Then the visitor is given a password, which they use to enter the site. This way the website can track their visits, greet them with a personal message and send them e-mails telling them about new developments.

Advertising

Running a website can be expensive and one way to offset some of the costs is to organize website advertising. Many sites have advertising banners, which offer the visitor the chance to visit the home site of the advertiser with a click on the banner. The advertiser usually pays the website according to the number of people who click on the banner.

Running for awards

There are a number of organizations that examine websites and give them awards. A well-designed site can be entered for web awards in order to increase the visibility of the site. Another good way of attracting a steady stream of visitors is to make sure that the site is child-friendly. This means that it will qualify for inclusion in the children-friendly listings. These search engines check all the sites that they recommend so that parents can be reassured that they are safe for their children to visit.

Keeping it fresh

There may be a lot of visitors during the first few weeks of going **on-line**, but the numbers can drop back after a while. People only revisit a site if they find it interesting, so it is very important to keep adding new content to the website. This might include the latest edition of the magazine, updates on campaigns or new items to buy, and will help ensure that the visitor sees something new each time they visit.

Many web pages display logos to indicate that they have won awards, that they are members of a particular organization or that they have met certain standards. These logos indicate that the website contains material that is safe for children to see.

On the job

Once a website is up and running, the day-to-day management is carried out by the webmaster. The most important skill for a webmaster is adaptability. Web visitors expect fresh and exciting material. The webmaster must learn about the new tools that become available and be familiar with **graphics** and multimedia software. The job is very varied and may include creating new content, adapting existing content, running the web server software, running other web-related software and performing system administration for the computer system that the web server runs on. Text for the site must be converted to **HTML**, while images have to be processed for size, **resolution** and format.

The role of cookies

ookies are packets of information that are sent by a web **server** to be stored on a user's computer and read back via the **browser** at a future point in time. This is useful, as it lets the browser retain some specific information, such as the fact that you have successfully used an ID and password to enter the site. Cookies are also used to store preferences of start pages – both Internet Explorer® and Netscape® Navigator use cookies to create personal start pages. Most **on-line** ordering systems use cookies to help remember what a person wanted to buy. For example, if a person spends an hour ordering goods at a particular site and suddenly there is a power cut or they have to switch off their browser, when they reconnect they will find that the items are still in their 'shopping basket'.

Users can set the preferences of their browser so that they get a message each time a server wants to set a cookie. This allows them to choose whether or not to accept the cookie.

The server www.bridgeman.co.uk wishes to set a cookie that will be sent only back to itself The name and value of the cookie are:
sesessionid=97437494615Jc1yvn-3X
Do you wish to allow the cookie to be set?

Cancel   OK

Cookies are also used for site personalization. For example, a visitor comes to a news site and is very interested in sports news. The site will allow the page to be personalized to show a panel containing sports headlines, and will set up cookies to ensure that the sports panel is automatically loaded when the site is visited in the future.

Better web design

One of the main uses of cookies is to track the path taken through a website by a visitor. This can help a web designer to improve the site layout. For example, cookies can reveal dead-end paths – places in the website that people go to and then leave because they do not have any more interesting links to hit. It can also give a more accurate count of how many people have been to the pages on the site. Cookies allow designers to distinguish between 50 different people visiting the site and just one person hitting the reload button 50 times.

Targeted marketing

Information from cookies can also be used for targeted marketing. The cookies provide information that is used to build up a profile of which pages were visited by a person and what advertisements they clicked on. The website then displays advertisements that they think will be of interest to this particular visitor on their next visit. This is something which is causing a lot of debate as a lot of people consider it to be an invasion of privacy. However, it is important to remember that cookies cannot be used to obtain **data** from a hard drive, or to get an **e-mail** address or steal personal information. Almost all browsers allow the user to reject cookies if they want, or pop up an alert box to warn the user that a server is trying to set a cookie.

www.tonystone.com

| HOME | FIND AND SELECT IMAGES | VIEW LIGHTBOXES | ACCOUNT OPTIONS | VIEW CURRENT ORDER | |

| Welcome | About Stone | Products and Services | New User Registration |

Welcome back Paul

Every week, we update our website with new images from our collection.

Begin your search here.

[Search] Advanced

[North America ▼] [go]

Photographs From

What's new?

O2

623

Play

[Past collections ▼] [go]

Sign in

Register or sign in here. You can also use a gettyone.com username and password to sign in.

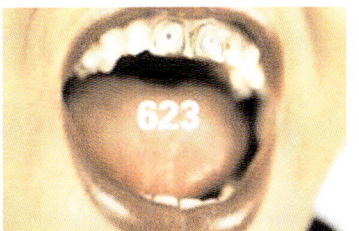

*By setting cookies, **websites** can send a personal message to a user each time they visit the site. Cookies may also reset the page, so, for example, images that were selected the last time the user visited the site are still stored in their 'image set'.*

A global market place

The Internet is growing fast. Every day, thousands of people log on to the Internet for the first time. Once new consumers in India and other parts of Asia, South America and Africa have access to the Internet, the global market will be truly colossal. It is becoming almost essential for a modern business to offer some form of **e-commerce** facilities to its customers, whether those customers are consumers or other businesses. Once a company has created a **website**, they almost automatically have a global business, for there are no international barriers on the Internet. You can buy goods or services from a company on the other side of the world and pay for it using an internationally recognized credit card. More than 20 million people are currently buying products and services through the Internet. In 1998, **on-line** retail shoppers spent close to $5 billion, and by 2001, on-line retail sales are expected to top $17.8 billion.

The pros and cons of on-line trading

Some of the items purchased on-line can even be delivered on-line. For example, software and music can be **downloaded** once purchased. But the majority of items have to be delivered to the purchaser's home or office and this is one of the largest drawbacks to on-line shopping. Many people who use the Internet to shop do so because they live in remote places or work long hours and cannot get to the shops easily. Therefore, finding a time when they will be at home to receive the goods can be a problem. On-line purchases often incur delivery charges that can make the cost of a small item, such as a book or CD, no cheaper than buying it in the local shops, since delivery of single items is not particularly efficient. Over the last few years, national and international carriers have developed streamlined delivery schemes, making use of central depots, to keep the delivery system relatively cheap and efficient. The Internet allows many small traders to move lots of items, often from country to country. They cannot easily make use of large vehicles loading up at a central depot so, unless distribution systems improve, this may result in more vehicles on our roads.

Even if you order something on-line you have to rely on conventional delivery methods to receive your goods.

Interactive TVs and phones

At the moment, most e-commerce is carried out via the personal computer and only a few people have **interactive** TV, but this is changing. It is predicted that more and more people will use their TVs and other Internet-enabled devices, such as pagers and mobile phones, to send and receive **e-mail**, access the Web and carry out on-line transactions. We will become used to doing most of our banking on-line as well as our weekly food shopping. Soon, everything from cars to refrigerators will be connected to the network and able to communicate with each other. Electrolux, for example, has developed the Screenfridge, a 21st century Internet icebox that manages your food supplies, among other things. It can e-mail a shopping list to your cyber-supermarket and co-ordinate a convenient delivery time to fit in with your schedule.

*The latest generation of mobile phones are 'WAP-enabled'. This means that the user can receive news bulletins and access their **ISPs** to collect and send e-mail whilst on the move.*

Technical tips

Phone users can now access the Internet using WAP, or Wireless Application **Protocol**. The user can receive services such as news, sports and business lists. The main limitation is the small screen on which the user can view the information, so companies are working on how to present information for WAP connections. Wireless technology will also be incorporated into the new generation of cars, connecting drivers to their offices and homes via the Internet.

A changing society

Recent studies have found that the more time people spend surfing the Internet, the less time they spend communicating with other people. In particular, 27 per cent of heavy Internet users reported spending less time talking to friends and family over the phone, 15 per cent reported spending less time physically with friends and family, while 13 per cent said they spent less time attending events outside their home.

The fact that people are spending longer at the computer and having less real contact with other people will affect societies. In the future, people will be more likely to communicate with other people via **e-mail** and video conference, rather than physically meeting face-to-face. They will have less need to leave their homes to watch movies or even to go shopping. They will be able to buy much of what they need **on-line**. The medical implications of this level of technological dependence are unknown, but some doctors have found that people who spend many hours at the computer are more likely to suffer from depression.

*Many children in developing countries do not have access to up-to-date resources, such as text books, because of the costs involved. Today, the **World Wide Web** allows more of these children access to a wealth of information. Schoolchildren around the world are in communication with each other, exchanging ideas and building friendships.*

Gallery

Examples of Reconstruction Images

(Click on any for a larger-size version)

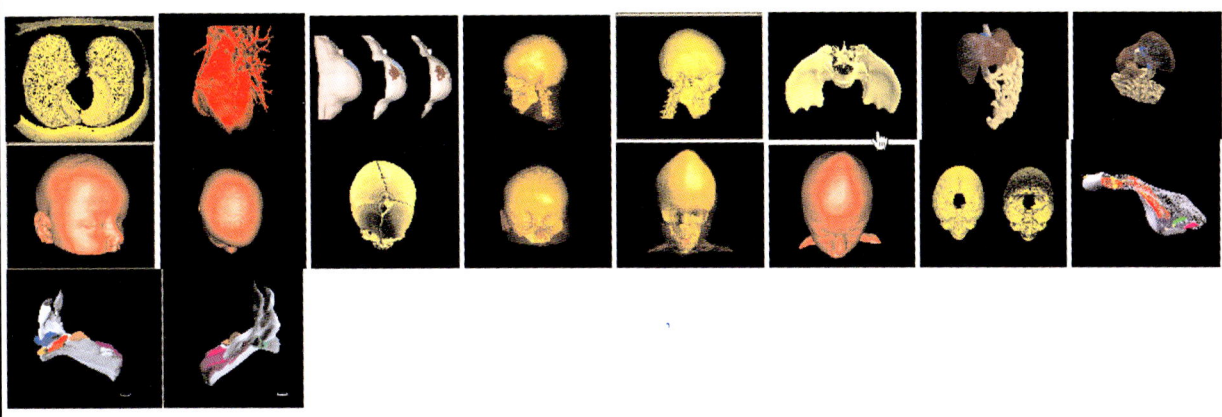

For more images and several mpeg animations, please click here: More images

Return to The Center for Bioinformatics Homepage: http://biocomp.arc.nasa.gov

Rei Cheng (reicheng@perseus.arc.nasa.gov)

One advantage of the trend is that the increase in the amount of business done on the Internet should benefit rural communities. No longer will it be important to live within commuting distance of the shops and offices. Today, some people 'telecommute' using the Internet, allowing them to make a choice of where to live based on quality of life, rather than proximity to work. Many cities view the Internet as part of the solution to the problems of clogged highways and foul air. Schools use the Internet as a vast electronic library, with untold educational possibilities. Doctors use the Internet to consult with colleagues on the other side of the world.

Sometimes, doctors in local hospitals are not able to carry out certain procedures because they have not had the right training or experience. Soon they will be able to practise new surgical techniques using a 'virtual surgery'. This will allow them to practise the techniques using a 'cyberscalpel' before they enter the operating room. These developments will mean that patients in remote places will get much better medical treatment. NASA plans to use this type of technology to provide health care to astronauts on long space journeys.

But, even as the Internet offers the potential of a single 'global village', it threatens to create second class citizens of those without access. As a new generation grows up, as accustomed to communicating through a keyboard as in person, life 'on the Net' will become an increasingly important part of life on Earth.

*Doctors and medical students can access **websites** which provide the latest medical information. On this site, users can find detailed anatomical **animations** that will help them to improve their surgical skills.*

Glossary

animation moving image

applet small Java program downloaded and run on your computer when a web page containing the program is accessed

bps bits per second. The amount of data sent and received per second. A bit is the smallest unit of computer data, it is either a 0 or 1. A byte is made up of 8 bits. A megabyte (MB) is a million bytes, or 8 million bits.

browser program that allows you to see and interact with web pages on the World Wide Web. The most widely used are Internet Explorer and Netscape Navigator.

compression making a file smaller so that it is quicker to transfer and takes up less storage space

data raw, unformatted information. Data can be anything from numbers to words.

database store of computerized information

decompression returning a compressed file to its original size

decrypt to decipher or unscramble a coded message

digital information stored in the form of the binary digits 0 and 1

digitize to convert into digital form

domain name official Internet name for a particular area of the Internet, such as elephantaid.org

download to copy a file from one computer to another, typically from a web server to your own

e-commerce (electronic commerce) the buying and selling of goods and services across the Internet

e-mail (electronic mail) the sending of electronic messages from one computer to another over the Internet. An e-mail address usually consists of a user ID and a domain name, separated by the @ sign (for example john.smith@companyname.com).

encoded put into code

encrypt to hide the meaning of a message by converting it into code

firewall a barrier, made of software and/or hardware, between two networks, which allows only authorized communication to pass

graphics visual elements on a web page, such as artwork and photographs

hacker person who gains illegal access to information stored on computers

home page the web page which is the entry point to a website

hyperlink pointer from a piece of text or graphics to a page or file on the World Wide Web, also called a link

HyperText Markup Language (HTML) language that uses a defined set of commands, known as tags, and text to create web pages

icon symbol or graphic on a web page that has a particular meaning and helps with navigation

interactive allowing the exchange of information between the user and the web page, or a web page that responds to inputs from the user

Internet Service Provider (ISP) company that provides access to the Internet by connecting users' computers via modem, ISDN and so on

Java programming language used to create small programs called applets. These applets may be contained within a web page.

JPEG (Joint Photographic Experts Group) format for compressing and storing images

modem device that connects your computer to another computer via a telephone line

navigation route around a website

on-line connected to the Internet

programmer person who writes the series, or lines, of coded instructions that make up a computer program

protocol rules or procedures that determine how computers interact with each other

real-time something that is taking place 'live', as you watch it

resolution (of images) the number of dots displayed per unit of printed length in an image, usually measured in dots per inch (dpi)

scan to make a digital copy of an image, page of writing or piece of artwork

server computer that stores information on the Internet. It might be a web server, a mail server or a database server.

tag 'label' or text string used in HTML to identify a page element's type, format or appearance, for example the colour of the text

Uniform Resource Locator (URL) the Internet address of a web page on the World Wide Web

upload to send files to another computer

usability how easy something is to use

virus piece of software that replicates (reproduces) itself on to other people's systems via transfer of data between computers. Many are designed to damage the computer's hard drive and files.

website collection of web pages linked together by a common topic or theme

World Wide Web the collection of interconnecting web pages that forms a global source of information

Index

Titles in the *Behind Media* series include:

Hardback   0 431 11450 1

Hardback   0 431 11452 8

Hardback   0 431 11463 3

Hardback   0 431 11461 7

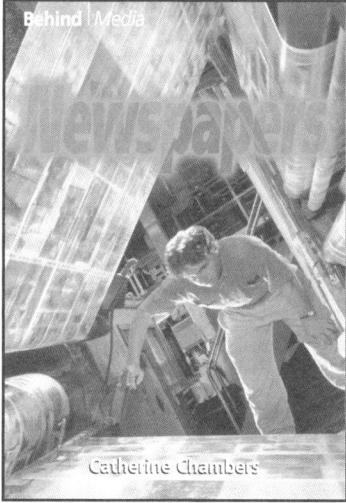

Hardback   0 431 11460 9

Hardback   0 431 11462 5

Hardback   0 431 11451 X

Hardback   0 431 11453 6

Find out about other Heinemann books on our website www.heinemann.co.uk/library